THE FIVE SENSES
Hearing

by Lisa Owings

BLASTOFF!
3
READERS

BELLWETHER MEDIA • MINNEAPOLIS, MN

Note to Librarians, Teachers, and Parents:

Blastoff! Readers are carefully developed by literacy experts and combine standards-based content with developmentally appropriate text.

Level 1 provides the most support through repetition of high-frequency words, light text, predictable sentence patterns, and strong visual support.

Level 2 offers early readers a bit more challenge through varied simple sentences, increased text load, and less repetition of high-frequency words.

Level 3 advances early-fluent readers toward fluency through increased text and concept load, less reliance on visuals, longer sentences, and more literary language.

Level 4 builds reading stamina by providing more text per page, increased use of punctuation, greater variation in sentence patterns, and increasingly challenging vocabulary.

Level 5 encourages children to move from "learning to read" to "reading to learn" by providing even more text, varied writing styles, and less familiar topics.

Whichever book is right for your reader, Blastoff! Readers are the perfect books to build confidence and encourage a love of reading that will last a lifetime!

This edition first published in 2018 by Bellwether Media, Inc.

No part of this publication may be reproduced in whole or in part without written permission of the publisher. For information regarding permission, write to Bellwether Media, Inc., Attention: Permissions Department, 5357 Penn Avenue South, Minneapolis, MN 55419.

Library of Congress Cataloging-in-Publication Data

Names: Owings, Lisa, author.
Title: Hearing / by Lisa Owings.
Description: Minneapolis, MN : Bellwether Media, Inc., 2018. | Series: Blastoff! Readers. The Five Senses | Audience: Age 5-8. | Audience: K to Grade 3. | Includes bibliographical references and index.
Identifiers: LCCN 2017029553 | ISBN 9781626177680 (hardcover : alk. paper) | ISBN 9781618912961(pbk. : alk. paper) | ISBN 9781681034775 (ebook)
Subjects: LCSH: Hearing–Juvenile literature. | Ear–Juvenile literature. | Senses and sensation–Juvenile literature.
Classification: LCC QP462.2 .O95 2018 | DDC 612.8/5–dc23
LC record available at https://lccn.loc.gov/2017029553

Editor: Christina Leaf   Designer: Lois Stanfield

Printed in the United States of America, North Mankato, MN.

3 1813 00597 3549

Table of Contents

The Parade Is Coming!

Excited voices rise and fall
around you. You make your way
to the curb. The crowd cheers as
the first floats roll past.

A drumbeat begins down the street. Everyone turns toward the sound.

The sound grows until it shakes your whole body. Then the band begins playing.

You hear the **bass** of tubas and the high **trills** of flutes. This is your favorite part of the parade!

What Is Hearing?

Our ears allow us to hear music, speech, and other sounds.

We can hear whispers and bangs, piercing screams and low hums. Each sound is a **vibration** that moves through the air in waves.

The outer ear is the part of the ear we can see. It is shaped like a funnel.

outer ear

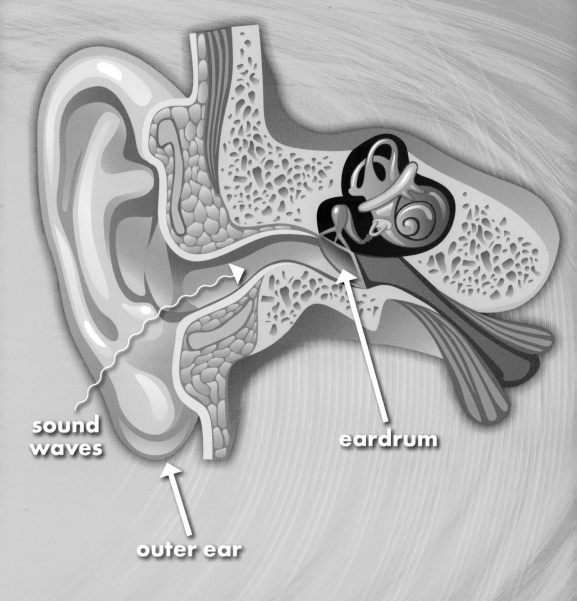

**sound
waves**

eardrum

outer ear

This part collects sound
waves. It guides them in
toward the **eardrum**.

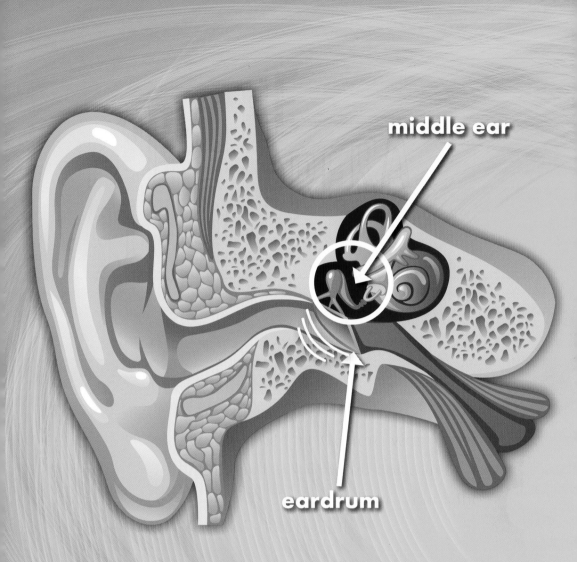

middle ear

eardrum

The eardrum vibrates as sound waves push against it. Each vibration then passes through a chain of tiny bones in the middle ear.

These bones are the hammer, anvil, and stirrup.

stirrup

hammer

anvil

eardrum

sound waves

13

The stirrup knocks against the inner ear. This sends waves through **fluid** in the **cochlea**.

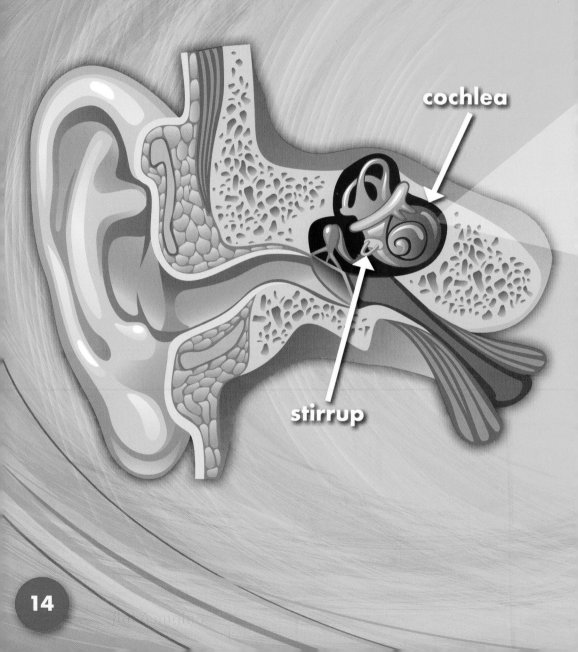

cochlea

stirrup

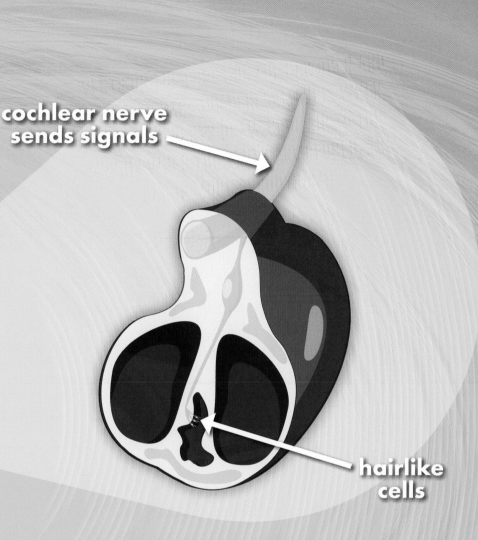

cochlear nerve
sends signals

hairlike
cells

As waves travel through this **coiled** tube, hairlike cells within the cochlea move. Their movements create **signals** that the brain reads as sounds.

When we cannot use our eyes, we often depend on our ears. Hearing taught early humans to hunt and **communicate** using sounds.

Sounds also warn us
of danger. We can
hear a car coming or
a fire alarm.

Hearing tells us where things are. Loud thunder means the storm is close! The thunder gets fainter as the storm moves away.

Sometimes we hear more sound through one ear. Then we know the sound is closer to that ear.

Our ears are especially good at understanding speech. We listen for words and other cues. We can tell how someone feels just by their tone. Take a moment to listen to the world around you!

Find That Sound!

Try this activity to see how location affects sound!

Sit slightly away from a wall. Close your eyes. Have a friend clap from different spots in the room.

- Can you point to where each sound is coming from?

Next, hold one ear closed. Repeat the activity.

- What differences do you notice?

Finally, plug both ears.

- Can you still hear your friend clapping?

- Can you tell from where?

Glossary

bass—deep or low tones

cochlea—a tube inside the inner ear that is coiled like a snail shell; within the cochlea, waves change into signals that the brain understands as sounds.

coiled—wound into a spiral shape

communicate—to share information, usually using speech or body language

eardrum—a thin piece of skin between the outer and middle ear; the eardrum vibrates when sound waves hit it.

fluid—a substance that is able to flow

signals—electrical messages sent to the brain

trills—musical sounds in which two notes are repeated quickly several times

vibration—something that moves back and forth quickly

To Learn More

AT THE LIBRARY

Lay, Kathryn. *Hearing Their Prey: Animals with an Amazing Sense of Hearing.* Minneapolis, Minn.: Magic Wagon, 2013.

Spilsbury, Louise and Richard. *Shhh! Listen: Hearing Sounds.* Chicago, Ill.: Heinemann Library, 2014.

Uhlberg, Myron. *The Sound of All Things.* Atlanta, Ga.: Peachtree Publishers, 2016.

ON THE WEB

Learning more about hearing is as easy as 1, 2, 3.

1. Go to www.factsurfer.com.

2. Enter "hearing" into the search box.

3. Click the "Surf" button and you will see a list of related web sites.

With factsurfer.com, finding more information is just a click away.

Index

The images in this book are reproduced through the courtesy of: Burlingham, Cover; dashingstock, pp. 4-5, 5; Png Studio Photography, pp. 5, 6, 7; Piti Tan, p. 8; Alexander Pekour, p. 9; BLACKDAY, p. 10; Sedova Elena, pp. 11, 12, 14; QAI Publishing, p. 13; Mister_X, p. 15; Akemaster, pp. 16-17; r.classen, p. 17 (top); Sergey Ryzhov, p. 17 (bottom); Shane Wilson, pp. 18-19; wavebreakmedia, p. 19; Iakov Fillimonov, p. 20; YAKOBCHUK VIACHESLAV, p. 21 (top); Olga Sapegina, p. 21 (bottom).